S0-AGE-999

Pet Corner

MARVELOUS MICE

By Rose Carraway

 **Gareth Stevens**
Publishing

Please visit our website, www.garethstevens.com. For a free color catalog of all our high-quality books, call toll free 1-800-542-2595 or fax 1-877-542-2596.

Library of Congress Cataloging-in-Publication Data

Carraway, Rose.
Marvelous mice / Rose Carraway.
   p. cm. — (Pet corner)
Includes index.
ISBN 978-1-4339-6299-8 (pbk.)
ISBN 978-1-4339-6300-1 (6-pack)
ISBN 978-1-4339-6297-4 (library binding)
1. Mice as pets—Juvenile literature. I. Title.
SF459.M5C37 2012
636.935—dc23

                                        2011024745

First Edition

Published in 2012 by
Gareth Stevens Publishing
111 East 14th Street, Suite 349
New York, NY 10003

Copyright © 2012 Gareth Stevens Publishing

Editor: Katie Kawa
Designer: Andrea Davison-Bartolotta

Photo credits: Cover David De Lossy/Photodisc/Thinkstock; pp. 1, 21, 24 (lettuce) iStockphoto/Thinkstock; pp. 5, 11, 15, 19, 21, 23, 24 (lettuce, pellets) Shutterstock.com; pp. 7, 9, 13 iStockphoto.com; pp. 17, 24 (paws) Bob Elsdale/The Image Bank/Getty Images.

All rights reserved. No part of this book may be reproduced in any form without permission in writing from the publisher, except by a reviewer.

Printed in the United States of America

CPSIA compliance information: Batch #CW12GS: For further information contact Gareth Stevens, New York, New York at 1-800-542-2595.

Contents

Mice like to run!

5

A pet mouse has
a wheel in its cage.
It runs in the wheel.

7

A mouse has toys
to chew. This keeps
its teeth healthy.

Mice sleep during the day. They play at night.

Most pet mice are white.

13

Fancy mice are special pet mice. They come in lots of colors!

Mice clean themselves.
They lick their paws
and wipe their fur.

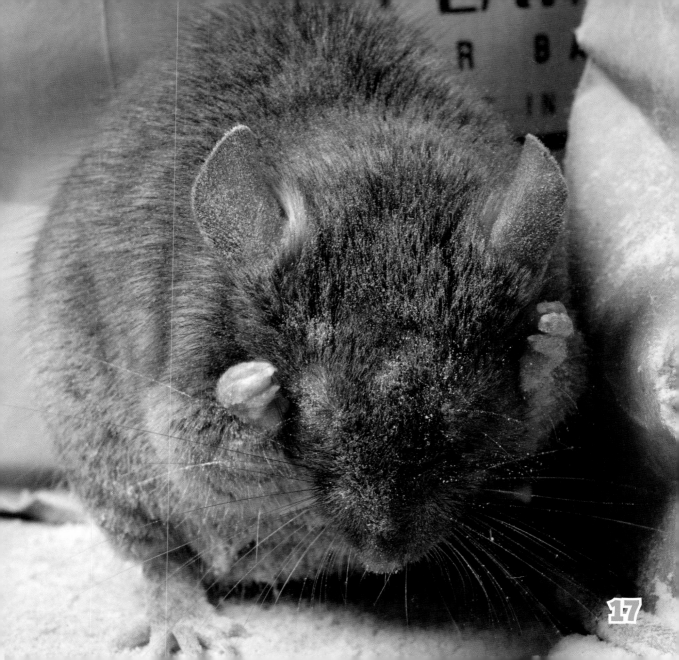

Pet mice eat food called pellets. These come from the pet store.

19

Mice eat green vegetables too. They like lettuce.

21

Mice learn tricks. They sit in a person's hand!

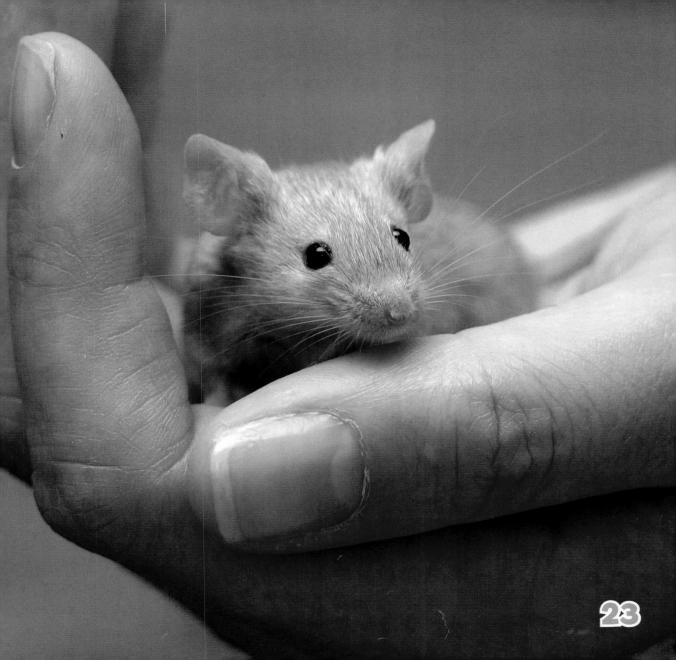

Words to Know

lettuce

paws

pellets

Index

CANCELLED

Westlake Porter Library
Westlake, OH 44145